Disclaimer

Food Handling: Please use great caution and sanitary practices when handling food products. Refer to your health department's safe food handling guidelines. Wash your hands and surfaces thoroughly before and after handling any food product.

The cooking instructions and directions in this book are offered as guidelines only. Use your best judgment and proper discretion when preparing or consuming any food.

We do not advise eating any eggs, meat or seafood that has not been properly handled or cooked. Eating something undercooked or raw is to be done at your own discretion.

We expressly disclaim responsibility for any adverse effect that may result from the use or application of the information contained in this book.

Limit of Liability and Disclaimer of Warranty: We have used our best efforts in preparing this book, and the information is provided "as is." We make no representation or warranties with respect to the accuracy or completeness of the contents of the cookbook and we specifically disclaim any implied warranties of merchantability or fitness for any particular purpose.

All material in this book is provided for your information only and may not be construed as medical advice or instruction. No action or inaction should be taken based solely on the contents of this information; instead, readers should consult appropriate health professionals on any matter relating to their health and well-being.

WE DO NOT CLAIM TO BE DOCTORS, NUTRITIONISTS OR DIETITIANS. THE INFORMATION IN THIS BOOK DOES IS MERELY OUR PERSONAL OPINION AND DOES NOT REPLACE PROFESSIONAL MEDICAL OR NUTRITIONAL ADVISE.

Contents

Introduction

As you let yourself get into cooking, you will be facing different challenges. These can be the recipe that you follow, the ingredients that you have, or might be the cooking utensils that you choose. In dealing all these stuffs, it is very important to let yourself be acquainted first about the different tactics in cooking.

There are cooking utensils that are also applicable in baking, and in making desserts. This is of a great help for you since, you can choose a lot of varieties that can make your cooking a successful one.

You have heard about the Cast Iron Skillet and its benefits to people. You have found out that it is adorable and durable though the price is quite surprising but it is all worth it.

This time, I will introduce you to some other uses of the Cast Iron Skillet and soon, you can find its multi-purpose means as well. In fact, the cast iron skillet is a great tool that serves as a guide for beginners. The following are the reasons for this.

BENEFITS

❖ You can control everything

The cast iron skillet offers a very special feature that you can utilize by using both the stovetop and in the oven. You can use this first in a stove before taking the next procedure in the oven. Because of this, your first baking and cooking experiences will be unforgettable like no other. You will arrive in a cooked food that truly suits your liking.

❖ Things are less messy

It has been discussed above that the Cast iron skillet is useful in a stovetop and in the oven. This further explains why it minimizes the accumulation of your sink since it keeps the file of mixing bowls orderly. Therefore, after your enjoyable baking and cooking routines, rest assured that your things are less messy and easy to clean up.

❖ It conserves heat

Cast iron skillet provides an even and constant heat because it has a high heat capacity. This further explains why some cook would love to use it in searing meat. This also applies in baking. It has the ability to ensure your cake's tenderness without burning its sweet sugary blaze.

If one of your dreams is to be a good baker, then I advise you to use the Cast iron skillet as your first choice. It can bring you enjoyment and excitement while cooking. With some awesome benefits mentioned above, you will be encouraging to engage in cooking and in baking using the Cast iron Skillet. Therefore, you are inspired to upgrade you cooking and baking skills a bit. There's nothing wrong to try a new. Use your cooking skills and choose the best cooking apparatus like the Cast iron skillet and things will go smoothly and orderly. Of course, you also need to follow the recipes that you have before taking your cooking dreams into an awesome reality.

Savory Dutch Baby

Prep time: 2 minutes
Cook time: 50 minutes
Total Time: 52 minutes
Serves: 4

INGREDIENTS

- 3 large eggs
- ¾ c whole milk
- 3 tbsp unsalted butter, slightly cooled, melted, divided
- ½ c all-purpose flour
- 2 tbsp cornstarch
- ½ tsp kosher salt
- ½ tsp freshly ground black pepper

INSTRUCTIONS

1. Place a medium ovenproof cast iron in the oven and preheat 450°. Let heat for about 25 minutes.
2. Blend eggs in a blender until frothy for 1 minute. While motor running, gradually stream 2 tbsp butter and milk blend for another 30 sec.
3. Add flour salt and pepper, and cornstarch then blends for another half a minute.
4. Carefully remove cast iron from oven and then swirl the remaining 1 tbsp butter as the coat. Immediately pour batter. Bake pancake until puffed and edges turned brown for about 20 minutes. It will deflate as soon as it comes out.
5. Top as desired and served.

Beef and Stout Skillet Pie

Prep time: 20 minutes
Cook time: 40 minutes
Total Time: 60 minutes
Serves: 4

INGREDIENTS

- 1 tbsp olive oil
- 1 pound Lean Ground Beef
- 4 ounce shiitake mushrooms
- Kosher salt and pepper
- 2 tablespoon tomato paste
- 1/2 cup frozen pearl onions
- 1 tablespoon fresh thyme leaves
- 3 tablespoon all-purpose flour
- 8 ounce stout
- 2 cup frozen butternut squash pieces
- 1 cup frozen peas
- 1 large egg
- 1 refrigerated rolled pie crust

INSTRUCTIONS

1. Heat oven to 375° F. Heat oil in your 9" cast iron over medium heat. Put the beef and mushrooms. Add ¾ tsp. salt and ¾ tsp pepper. Cook for 6 minutes by breaking up the beef. Discard any fat.
2. Add tomato paste and cook for 2 minutes. Add thyme, onions and sprinkle flour and stir for half a minute.
3. Add stout and simmer for 1 minute or until the liquid thickened. Add a half cup of water and simmer for about 1 minute. Add peas and squash then simmer again for another 1 minute. Remove from heat.
4. Place pastry by unrolling on the cutting board and brush with egg. Place dough with the egg-side up on the top of beef mixture. Press gently the edges.
5. Bake until golden brown for 35 minutes. Let rest before serving and enjoy.

Oven-Roasted Kimchi Chicken

Prep time: 15 minutes
Cook time: 50 minutes
Total Time: 65 minutes
Serves: 4

INGREDIENTS
Kimchi Butter
- 6 tbsp unsalted butter
- ⅓ c kimchi with 1 tbsp kimchi juice
- ¼ tsp kosher salt
- Chicken
- 2 tbsp coriander seeds
- 1 tsp crushed red pepper flakes
- 1 tsp grated lemon zest
- ½ tsp black peppercorns
- ¼ tsp cumin seeds
- 4 tsp kosher salt
- 1 3½ lb chicken, backbone removed
- 1 lb fingerling potatoes
- 4 oz thick-cut bacon, cut into 1" pieces
- 2 ears of corn, husked, cut crosswise into 3" pieces

INSTRUCTIONS

Kimchi Butter

1. Pulse the kimchi, kimchi juice, butter, and salt in a food processor. Scrape down the sides as needed until the mixture is fully incorporated.
2. Cover and store at room temperature. Kimchi butter can be done ahead of time and just chill.

Chicken

1. Put lemon zest, red pepper flakes, coriander seeds, cumin seeds, black peppercorns and 4 teaspoon salt in a spice mill with mortar and pepper. Grind until texture is very fine.
2. Place chicken on rimmed baking sheet. Press firmly the breastbone using your hand's heel to flatten. Season chicken with ¼ c spice mixture on both sides. Chill for 3-8 hours uncovered.
3. Boil potatoes for about 15 minutes in salted water or just tender. When done, remove from heat and let sit.
4. Preheat oven to 550°. Place half of the kimchi butter on your chicken and roast for 25 minutes.
5. Put potatoes, corn, and bacon around the chicken. Sprinkle with your remaining spice mixture. Insert an instant-read thermometer on the thigh part and roast until it registers 165° or about 15 minutes.
6. When done, place on a cutting board and let cool before carving.
7. Place the vegetables and bacon in a bowl and put the remaining kimchi butter. Toast to melt and coat the vegetables.
8. Serve alongside the chicken and enjoy.

Phyllo Pie with Kale, Butternut Squash and Goat Cheese

Prep time: 10 minutes
Cook time: 40 minutes
Total Time: 50 minutes
Serves: 4

INGREDIENTS

- 3 tbsp olive oil, (add more for brushing)
- 2 medium finely chopped red onions
- ½ small butternut squash, cut into ¾-inch pieces
- 1½ tsp chopped thyme
- ½ tsp crushed red pepper flakes
- 1 bunch Tuscan kale, sliced thinly crosswise, stems and ribs removed
- 2 large beaten and blend eggs
- 3 oz grated Parmesan
- 1 tsp grated lemon zest
- salt and pepper
- 8 oz frozen phyllo pastry, thawed
- 4 oz fresh goat cheese, crumbled

INSTRUCTIONS

1. Preheat oven to 400°. Heat the oil in cast iron over medium. Add onions and cook for 8 minutes or until brown.
2. Add squash and stir occasionally until almost tender for 10 minutes. Add red pepper, thyme, and flakes. Then transfer to a bowl and let it cool. Wipe out the cast iron and reserve.
3. Add lemon zest, parmesan, eggs, and kale to your squash mixture and combine. Add salt and pepper.
4. Layer phyllo sheet on your reserved cast iron. Spoon the mixture into phyllo and top with goat cheese. Brush with oil on the edges of your phyllo. Fold over filling and overlap slight leaving the center exposed.
5. Cook the mixture over medium heat for 3 minutes or until the bottom is just golden. Transfer the cast iron to oven and bake until crisp for about 25 minutes.
6. Let cool before slicing into wedges and serve.

Roast Chicken with Caramelized Leeks

Prep time: 10 minutes
Cook time: 60 minutes
Total Time: 70 minutes
Serves: 4

INGREDIENTS

- 1 3½ whole chicken
- Kosher salt and pepper
- 3 leeks, pale green and white parts only, halved lengthwise
- 3 tbsp olive oil, divided

INSTRUCTIONS

1. Using your paper towels, pat chicken to dry. Season with salt in and out. Tie the legs together and let sit for an hour, allowing the salt to penetrate.
2. Place rack in the upper third of your oven and insert your 12' cast iron and preheat the oven to 425 degrees.
3. Toss leeks and half of your oil in a bowl to coat, then season with salt and pepper.
4. Pat your chicken dry again and rub the remaining oil. Drizzle remaining oil into your hot skillet and place the chicken with the leeks around.
5. Roast until leeks are browned and an instant-read thermometer registers 165° or about an hour. Let chicken rest for half an hour.
6. Transfer chicken to the cutting board and then carve. Serve with leeks and enjoy.

Schmaltz-Refried Pinto Beans

Prep time: 10 minutes
Cook time: 110 minutes
Total Time: 120 minutes
Serves: 8

INGREDIENTS

- 3 oz slab bacon, sliced ¼ "thick
- 1 large chopped onion
- 4 cloves chopped garlic
- ¼ tsp crushed red pepper flakes
- ½ tsp ground cumin
- 1½ c dried pinto beans, soaked overnight
- Kosher salt and pepper
- ⅓ c schmaltz
- 1 tsp apple cider vinegar

INSTRUCTIONS

1. Cook bacon in a saucepan over medium heat. Turn often for a slightly crisp and browned for about 10 minutes.
2. Add garlic and onions, stirring occasionally for 10 minutes. Add red pepper flakes and cumin and cook for 1 minute.
3. Add 4 cups of water and beans, then bring to boil, reduce the heat and then cover. Stirring occasionally and add water if needed until beans are tender for 90 minutes. zTo taste season with salt and pepper and let sit to absorb the seasoning.
4. Heat the schmaltz in a skillet over medium. Add the beans mixture and mash using potato masher until beans are smooth and thick.Add vinegar and season salt and pepper to taste.
5. Serve and enjoy.

Skillet Fried Chicken

Prep time: 10 minutes
Cook time: 30 minutes
Total Time: 40 minutes
Serves: 4

INGREDIENTS

- 2 tbsp kosher salt, divided
- 2 tsp plus 1 tbsp pepper
- 1 1/2 tsp paprika
- 1/2 tsp garlic powder
- 3/4 tsp cayenne pepper
- 1/2 tsp onion powder
- 1 3-4 pounds chicken, cut into 10 pcs, remove backbone and wing tips
- 1 c buttermilk
- 3 c all-purpose flour
- 1 large egg
- 1 tbsp cornstarch
- Peanut oil to fry

INSTRUCTIONS

1. Whisk half of your salt and 2 teaspoons black pepper, garlic, cayenne, paprika and onion powder in a bowl. Season chicken with spices mixture and place in a bowl and chill overnight (covered).
2. Let the chicken stand at a room temperature for an hour. Whisk egg, half cup of water and buttermilk in a bowl. Whisk cornstarch, flour and the remaining salt and pepper in a baking dish.
3. Pour oil in your cast iron skillet. Prop deep-fry thermometer in the oil, heat over medium-high until it registers 350 degrees. Set a wire rack in your rimmed baking sheet.
4. Dip Chicken in the buttermilk mixture and dredge in the flour mixture. Place 5 pcs of chicken in the skillet and fry turning each side for 2 minutes. An instant-read thermometer inserted and registers 165° on the thickest part of the chicken for about 10 minutes.
5. Remove chicken and drip excess oil. Transfer to the prepared rack and let cool before serving.

Roast Chicken with Harissa and Schmaltz

Prep time: 10 minutes
Cook time: 50 minutes
Total Time: 60 minutes
Serves: 4

INGREDIENTS

- 3 garlic cloves, chopped
- ⅓ c sugar
- ¼ c coriander seeds
- 1 c kosher salt
- 1 4 lb chicken, halved, remove the backbone
- 1 c Harissa
- ¼ c schmaltz

INSTRUCTIONS

1. In a saucepan put 8 cups of water, kosher salt, coriander seeds, sugar, and garlic. Bring to a boil, stirring occasionally until the sugar and salt dissolved. Transfer to a bowl and add a cup of ice.
2. Bone the chicken breast while leaving the thigh and leg quarters intact, then cut off the wing tips and discard. Separate the rib cage from the flesh by cutting using a thin sharp knife. The only remaining bone is in the wing, drumstick, and thigh.
3. Place the chicken in your brine and cover, then chill for half a day.
4. Transfer chicken to baking pan and pick off the coriander seeds.Spread the harissa all over your chicken and chill for at least an hour.
5. Preheat oven to 400°. Heat the schmaltz in a cast iron over medium. Place the chicken with skin sides down. Cook until the skin starts to crisp for about 5 minutes. Transfer the cast iron to oven cook chicken until skin is dark and meat is cooked halfway for about 25 minutes.
6. Remove the cast iron and turn the chicken, the skin side up. Return to the oven and cook for 15 minutes or an instant-read thermometer registers 165 degrees.
7. Transfer chicken to a platter and drizzle with schmaltz and serve.

Cast-Iron Skillet Cornbread

Prep time: 5 minutes
Cook time: 40 minutes
Total Time: 45 minutes
Serves: 8

INGREDIENTS

- 1¼ c all-purpose flour
- 1 c fine-grind cornmeal
- 1 tbsp baking powder
- 1½ tsp kosher salt
- 4 large eggs
- 1½ c canned creamed corn
- 1 4.5 oz canned mild green chiles, drained and chopped
- 1½ oz mild white grated cheddar
- 1½ oz grated Monterey Jack
- ¾ c unsalted butter
- ⅔ c sugar
- Nonstick vegetable oil spray

INSTRUCTIONS

1. Place a rack in the middle of the oven. Set a cast iron on a rimmed baking sheet, and place over the rack then preheat the oven to 400 degrees.
2. Whisk salt, baking powder, cornmeal and flour in a bowl to mix. In a different bowl beat the eggs and whisk Monterey Jack, cheddar, chiles and creamed corn to combine.
3. In a large bowl mix the sugar and butter, then add the egg mixture. Mix in the dry ingredients.
4. Remove cast iron from the iron and coat with non-stick oil spray. Scrape in the batter slightly mounded in the middle and bake cornbread until golden brown for 40 minutes.
5. Let cool before serving.

One-Skillet Chicken with Buttery Orzo

Prep time: 5 minutes
Cook time: 40 minutes
Total Time: 45 minutes
Serves: 4

INGREDIENTS

- salt and pepper
- 6 chicken thighs, with skin and bones (patted dry)
- 3 tbsp unsalted butter, divided
- 1 chopped fennel bulb, plus chopped fronds
- 1 chopped leek, pale green and white parts only
- 8 oz orzo
- ⅓ c dry white wine
- 2½ low-sodium chicken broth, divided
- 1 tbsp fresh lemon juice
- 1 tsp grated lemon zest

INSTRUCTIONS

1. Preheat oven to 400 degrees. Season chicken with salt and pepper. In your cast iron, heat 2 tablespoon butter over medium-high. Place in the chicken in your cast iron with skin side down and no gaps in a single layer. Cook meat for 8 minutes or until the color is golden brown. Turn chicken with skin side up. Transfer to oven and bake for 15 minutes. Transfer to a platter.
2. In your cast iron put the leek and fennel bulb then combine and season with salt and pepper. Cook for 5 minutes or until leek is golden brown. Add orzo and cook for 3 minutes or until pasta is darkened.
3. Pour wine and stir until the liquid evaporates. Add broth half cup at a time and stir occasionally. Let the broth absorb before adding again and cook for 15 minutes.
4. Remove cast iron from heat. Add more salt and pepper according to your taste. Combine the lemon juice and the remaining butter then the chopped fennel fronds and mix. Put the chicken over and top with lemon zest.
5. Remove skillet from heat, Taste and add more salt and pepper to your liking; mix in lemon juice and remaining 1 Tbsp. butter, then chopped fennel fronds. Pile chicken on top and finish with lemon zest.

Raspberry Skillet Jam

Prep time: 5 minutes
Cook time: 20 minutes
Total Time: 25 minutes
Serves: 5

INGREDIENTS

- 2 pints of raspberries or blackberries
- 1 tablespoon of fresh lemon juice or lime juice
- ½ cup of sugar

INSTRUCTIONS

1. Combine raspberries and sugar in a medium cast-iron while mashing it with a wooden spoon to release the juices.
2. Stir over in a medium heat until its mixture thickens.
3. To see if the jam is set up properly, test it by spooning a bit on a plate.
4. Once it is chilled already, it should be slightly jelled.
5. Cook for another 5 mins. if it still syrupy.
6. Transfer the jam in a container or glass jar and keep refrigerated.

Cast-Iron Pizza with Fennel and Sausage

Prep time: 5 minutes
Cook time: 35 minutes
Total Time: 40 minutes
Serves: 2

INGREDIENTS

- 12 oz. store-bought pizza dough
- ½ small fennel bulb (thinly sliced)
- Kosher salt
- ⅓ cup prepared marinara
- 5 tbsp extra-virgin olive oil
- 8 oz. sweet Italian sausage
- ¾ cup coarsely grated low-moisture mozzarella
- 3 garlic cloves (thinly sliced)
- torn basil leaves and crushed red pepper flakes

INSTRUCTIONS

1. Place a rack on a topmost position of oven and preheat to 475°.
2. Place a dough on a work surface and drizzle with 1 tbsp of oil, turning into a coat.
3. In a large cast-iron, heat 1 tbsp oil.
4. Cook the sausages and break it up into small pieces. Transfer to a bowl after.
5. Remove the cast-iron from heat and lay the dough inside it carefully.
6. Season it with salt and spread marinara in the entire surface of the dough.
7. Top it with fennel, cooked sausage, garlic, and mozzarella.
8. Drizzle with 2 tablespoons of oil.
9. Check if the bottom if is already crisp and golden brown if not, set over medium-low and cook until it is already golden brown.
10. Carefully transfer cast iron to oven and bake the pizza on top rack until the crust is golden brown and cheese is bubbling over.
11. Cool it for 5 mins.
12. Top it with basil and red pepper flakes
13. Sprinkle more salt and drizzle it with 1 tbsp of oil.

Skillet Peach Cobbler

Prep time: 10 minutes
Cook time: 50 minutes
Total Time: 60 minutes
Serves: 5

INGREDIENTS

- 2 tsp salt
- 2 c all-purpose flour
- 2 large eggs (beaten)
- 1 ½ cup sugar
- 2 tsp baking powder
- 1 ½ c crème fraîche (divided)
- 1 c whole milk
- 1 c chilled heavy cream
- 2 tsp vanilla extract
- ¼ cup unsalted butter
- 2 tsp sugar
- 2 lb peeled peaches (cut into 1/2 inch wedges)
- 1 c Peach Preserve

INSTRUCTIONS

1. Preheat oven to 350°.
2. In a medium bowl, beat 1/2 cup crème fraîche, eggs, vanilla and milk.
3. Add the mixture to dry ingredients and beat until it's smooth.
4. In a 12 inch cast-iron melt the butter in a medium heat. Swirl until pan is coated with butter. Remove from heat after.
5. Add batter to pan and spread peaches over. Spoon dollops of preserves equally over batter.
6. Bake until a tester that was inserted in the middle of cobbler comes out clean.
7. For the meantime, put cream in a bowl and form soft peaks.
8. Then fold in the remaining 1 cup crème fraîche and sugar.
9. Carefully cut cobbler into wedges.
10. Serve it with a whipped cream mixture.

Cast- Iron Roast Chicken

Prep time: 6 minutes
Cook time: 45 minutes
Total Time: 51 minutes
Serves: 4

INGREDIENTS
- 1 3½-4lb whole chicken
- 1 tbsp olive oil
- Kosher salt

INSTRUCTIONS

1. Dry chicken using paper towels and then season with salt.
2. Tie the legs together and let sit 1hr to allow the salt to penetrate.
3. Place a rack in the upper third of the oven and set a three quart cast-iron baking dish on a rack.
4. Preheat the oven to 425°.
5. Dry chicken with paper towels and evenly coat with half of the oil.
6. Put remaining oil into cast-iron skillet. Place chicken and roast.
7. Let chicken rest in the skillet for 45 mins.
8. Slowly put the chicken on a cutting board and carve the legs off and breasts after.

Skillet Chicken Pot Pie with Butternut Squash

Prep time: 10 minutes
Cook time: 60 minutes
Total Time: 70 minutes
Serves: 6

INGREDIENTS

- 1 tbsp chopped sage
- ¼ c all-purpose flour
- 4 garlic cloves (chopped)
- ¼ c olive oil
- 1 c frozen white pearl onions
- 1 small bunch kale, center ribs removed (leaves chopped)
- salt and pepper
- 3 c chicken broth
- ½ small butternut squash (peeled and cut into ½" pcs)
- ½ rotisserie chicken (bite-size pcs)
- 1 sheet frozen puff pastry (thawed)
- 1 large egg

INSTRUCTIONS

1. Carefully place rack in upper third of the oven. Preheat to 425 degrees.
2. Heat oil in a heavy ovenproof cast-iron skillet over a medium-high heat.Saute' onions until it turns brown.
3. Reduce heat and put garlic. Saute' until it becomes brown.
4. Put kale and season it with pepper and salt. Continue cooking and sprinkle flour over and cook.
5. Stir in broth, ½-cupful at a time and add squash.Boil and reduce heat until squash is softened.
6. Put the chicken in skillet, stir and season with pepper and salt.
7. Carefully unfold pastry and smooth remaining creases. place over the skillet letting the corners to hang over the sides.
8. Whisk the egg and 1 tsp water in a bowl. Brush pastry with the egg wash and cut one-inch slits in top.
9. Bake pot pie until the pastry is beginning to turn brown.
10. Reduce heat temperature of the oven to 375° and cook until pastry is crisp and turns to golden brown.
11. Cool for 10 mins before serving.

Skillet- Baked Eggs with Yogurt, Chili oil and Spinach

Prep time: 10 minutes
Cook time: 25 minutes
Total Time: 35 minutes
Serves: 4

INGREDIENTS

- 1 tsp fresh lemon juice
- 2 tbsp olive oil
- Kosher salt
- 4 large eggs
- 2/3 c plain Greek-style yogurt
- 1 garlic clove (cut into halves)
- 2 tbsp unsalted butter (divided)
- 3 tbsp chopped leek (pale-green parts and white parts)
- 2 tbsp chopped scallion (pale-green parts and white parts)
- 10 c fresh spinach
- 1/4 tsp chili powder or 1/4 teaspoon crushed red pepper flakes
- 1 tsp chopped fresh oregano

INSTRUCTIONS

1. Mix garlic, yogurt and a bit of salt in a bowl. Set aside.
2. Preheat oven to 300°. Melt 1 tbsp of butter with oil in a cast-iron over a medium heat.
3. Put scallion and leek. Reduce the heat to low and cook until it becomes soft.
4. Add lemon juice and spinach; season with a bit of salt. Increase the heat to medium-high and then cook until wilted.Turn it frequently.
5. Carefully transfer spinach mixture to a 10" skillet leaving excess liquid behind.
6. Mix yogurt, garlic, and a pinch of salt in a small bowl. Set aside.
7. Make four deep indentations in the center of spinach in a larger skillet.
8. Break 1 egg into hollow, keep yolks intact.Bake until egg whites are set.
9. Melt the remaining butter in a saucepan over medium-low heat.
10. Add chili powder and a bit of salt. Cook until butter starts to foam.
11. Add oregano and cook for just half a minute.
12. Remove garlic from yogurt.
13. Put yogurt over spinach and eggs.
14. Lastly, drizzle with spiced butter.

Cornbread with caramelized Apples and Onions

Prep time: 5 minutes
Cook time: 45 minutes
Total Time: 50 minutes
Serves: 8

INGREDIENTS

- 1½ c cornmeal
- ¾ c plus 2 tbsp unsalted butter
- 1 med thinly sliced onion
- 1½ c buttermilk
- 1 tsp kosher salt
- 2 med thinly sliced red- or pink-skinned apples
- 5 tbsp sugar (divided)
- 3 tsp fresh thyme leaves (divided)
- 1 c all-purpose flour
- 1 tbsp baking powder
- ground black pepper
- 2 large eggs

INSTRUCTIONS

1. Preheat oven to 400°.
2. Pour all 2 tbsp butter in a small bowl and set aside.
3. Melt the butter in a skillet over medium-high heat.
4. Add onion, season with salt and pepper, and cook. Stir occasionally until onion is translucent and starts to turn brown. Transfer in a medium bowl after
5. Whisk flour, cornmeal 1 tsp salt, baking powder and 3 tbsp of sugar in a large bowl.
6. Slowly whisk eggs, buttermilk and ¾ c reserved melted butter until smooth.
7. Fold in half of the onion mixture and scrape batter into skillet.
8. Top with the remaining onion mixture and 1 tsp thyme.
9. Bake the cornbread until color is golden brown.
10. Let cool slightly before serving.

Reuben Dutch Baby

Prep time: 5 minutes
Cook time: 18 minutes
Total Time: 23 minutes
Serves: 4

INGREDIENTS

- 4 large eggs
- ½ c all-purpose flour
- ½ c milk
- 1 tsp Dijon mustard (add more for serving)
- ½ tsp freshly ground black pepper (add more)
- salt
- 4 oz coarsely grated Swiss cheese (divided)
- 8 oz pastrami (thinly sliced and divided)
- 2 tbsp unsalted butter
- Sauerkraut (for serving)

INSTRUCTIONS

1. Remove preheated skillet from oven. Add butter.
2. Swirl to coat butter into skillet.
3. Drape 4 oz of pastrami into skillet and season with salt and pepper.
4. Pour the egg mixture over.
5. Carefully return skillet to the oven and bake until the Dutch baby is already puffed and golden brown.
6. Remove skillet from oven and heat broiler.
7. Drape the remaining pastrami over the Dutch baby and top it with the remaining cheese.
8. Broil until cheese is melted.
9. Lastly, top it with sauerkraut and mustard before serving.

Cornmeal Biscuits with Scallions and Chorizo Gravy

Prep time: 10 minutes
Cook time: 36 minutes
Total Time: 46 minutes
Serves: 4

INGREDIENTS

- ¾ c buttermilk
- 1 c all-purpose flour
- 1 tbsp sugar
- ¾ c cornmeal
- 1½ tsp baking powder
- 1 tsp baking soda
- 1 tsp kosher salt
- ¼ tsp ground black pepper
- ½ c or 1 stick chilled unsalted butter (cut into pieces)

Gravy and Assembly

- hot sauce
- Kosher salt
- 1 tbsp vegetable oil
- 1 lb fresh chorizo (casings already removed)
- 3 tbsp all-purpose flour
- 2½ c whole milk
- freshly ground pepper
- 2 radishes (thinly sliced)
- 4 scallions (thinly sliced)
- ½ cup Cotija cheese
- 1 avocado (sliced)
- ½ cup cilantro leaves (with tender stems only)

INSTRUCTIONS

Biscuits
1. Preheat oven to 425°.
2. Combine cornmeal, sugar, baking soda, baking powder, salt, pepper and flour in a large bowl.
3. Work butter into flour until the pieces are already chickpea size; using your hands.
4. Add buttermilk and mix to blend.
5. Put dough by heaping ¼ cupful into an 8" cast-iron skillet, about 1" apart.
6. Bake, until biscuits, are golden brown, puffed and cooked through.

Gravy and Assembly
1. While waiting for the biscuits to bake, heat oil in a medium skillet over medium heat.
2. Add chorizo. Stir occasionally breaking up any large pieces. Cook until chorizo is crisp and browned.
3. Transfer to a bowl.
4. Whisk flour into drippings in a skillet and cook, whisking continuously until roux is turning light golden brown and very smooth.
5. Gradually add milk, whisking constantly until incorporated.
6. Reduce heat to medium-low and cook gravy, whisking constantly until thickened.
7. Stir half of the chorizo into the gravy, seasoning with pepper, hot sauce, and salt.
8. Spoon some gravy over hot biscuits and top with scallions, cilantro, radishes, remaining chorizo, Cotija, cheese and more hot sauce.
9. Serve with the remaining gravy alongside.

Pan-Roasted Chicken with Harissa Chickpeas

Prep time: 10 minutes
Cook time: 35 minutes
Total Time: 45 minutes
Serves: 4

INGREDIENTS

- Kosher salt
- 1 tbsp olive oil
- 2 tbsp tomato paste
- 8 bone-in chicken thighs (skin-on)
- 2 15-oz. cans chickpeas (rinsed)
- 1 small onion (finely chopped)
- 2 cloves garlic (finely chopped)
- ¼ c harissa paste
- ½ c low-sodium chicken broth
- ¼ c chopped fresh flat-leaf parsley
- Lemon wedges (for serving)
- Freshly ground pepper

INSTRUCTIONS

1. Preheat oven to 425°.
2. Heat oil in a large ovenproof skillet over medium-high.
3. Season chicken with salt and pepper.
4. Working with two batches, cook until browned and transfer to a plate.
5. Pour off 1 tbsp drippings from pan.
6. Add garlic and onion; cook and stir often until softened.
7. Then add tomato paste and cook. Stir, until it begins to darken.
8. Add broth, chickpeas, and harissa; simmer.
9. Nestle chicken, skin side up, in chickpeas; transfer skillet to oven.
10. Roast until chicken is cooked.
11. Top with parsley and serve with lemon wedges for squeezing over.

Cast-Iron Roast Chicken with Crispy Potatoes

Prep time: 5 minutes
Cook time: 100 minutes
Total Time: 105 mins
Serves: 4

INGREDIENTS
- salt and pepper
- 1 3½ lb whole chicken
- 1½ lb russet potatoes (thinly sliced crosswise)
- 2 tbsp unsalted butter, melted
- 2 tbsp olive oil (divided)
- 1 tbsp thyme leaves

INSTRUCTIONS

1. Dry chicken with paper towels and season generously with salt, inside and out.
2. Tie chicken legs with kitchen twine.
3. Let sit for 1 hr to allow the salt to penetrate.
4. Carefully place a rack in the upper third of oven and set a 12" cast-iron skillet.
5. Preheat oven 425°.
6. In a large bowl, toss potatoes, thyme, butter and 1 tbsp oil; season with pepper and salt.
7. When oven reaches temperature, dry chicken with paper towels and lightly coat with half of the remaining oil.
8. Drizzle the remaining oil into the hot skillet.
9. Place chicken in the middle of skillet and arrange potatoes around it.
10. Roast until potatoes are turning to golden brown and crisp.
11. Let chicken rest in skillet until slightly warm.
12. Transfer chicken to a cutting board and carve.
13. Serve with potatoes.

Cornmeal Hoecakes

Prep time: 2 minutes
Cook time: 18 minutes
Total Time: 20 minutes
Serves: 5

INGREDIENTS

- 2 tbsp sugar
- 1 c all-purpose flour
- ½ tsp kosher salt
- ¼ tsp baking powder
- ⅔ c coarse-grind cornmeal
- 1 large egg white
- 1 large egg
- 1¼ cups milk
- ¼ cup unsalted melted butter + 2 tsp
- Sour cream and sliced scallions (for serving)
- Flaky sea salt

INSTRUCTIONS

1. Preheat oven to 350°.
2. Whisk cornmeal, flour, kosher salt, sugar, and baking powder in a bowl.
3. Whisk egg, milk, and egg white in another bowl to combine.
4. Mix the mixture into your cornmeal mixture to incorporate, and then stir in the melted butter.
5. Heat 1 teaspoon butter in a cast-iron skillet over medium heat, swirling the pan to coat bottom.
6. Spoon in half of the batter and cook until the bubbles are can be seen on top.
7. Transfer cast-iron skillet to oven. Bake until the hoecake is set.
8. Return cast-iron skillet to the stovetop, turn the cake and cook over medium heat until firm.
9. Transfer to a plate. Repeat the process with the remaining batter and butter to make a second cake.
10. Serve hoecakes topped with scallions and sour cream and then sprinkled with sea salt.

Seeded Whole Grain Soda Bread

Prep time: 10 minutes
Cook time: 100 minutes
Total Time: 120 minutes
Serves: 5

INGREDIENTS

- ¼ c millet
- ¼ c quinoa
- 2 tbsp amaranth
- 3 tbsp brown rice syrup
- 3 c whole wheat flour
- 1 c all-purpose flour
- 1 c old-fashioned oats (plus more for topping)
- 2¼ cu buttermilk (divided) add more for brushing
- 1 tbsp vegetable oil (add more for pan)
- 2 tbsp flaxseed
- 1 tbsp kosher salt
- 2 tsp baking soda
- ¼ c sunflower seeds (add more for topping)
- 4 tbsp unsalted butter (cut into pcs)

INSTRUCTIONS

1. Mix quinoa, amaranth, millet, 1c buttermilk, 1c oats and ½ c water in a bowl. Cover then let sit for 8-12 hrs.
2. Preheat oven to 350°.
3. Lightly oil an 8" cast-iron skillet. Whisk salt, baking soda, all-purpose flour, whole wheat flour, flaxseed and ¼ c sunflower seeds in a large bowl.
4. Work in butter using fingers until largest pieces are pea-size.
5. Make a well in the enter and then add the brown rice syrup, oat mixture, 1 tbsp oil and 1 ¼ c buttermilk.
6. Mix until dough is smooth, slightly sticky.
7. Form a ball dough and place in prepared pan.
8. Brush with buttermilk; top with sunflower seeds and more oats.
9. Cut a large X on top and then bake until golden brown.
10. Let cool in pan.

Cast-Iron Roast Chicken with Winter Squash, Pancetta and Red Onions

Prep time: 7 minutes
Cook time: 120 minutes
Total Time: 127 minutes
Serves: 4

INGREDIENTS

- salt and pepper
- 2 tbsp unsalted butter (melted)
- 2 red onions (cut into wedges)
- 2 lb winter squash (cut into 1½-inch-thick wedges)
- 3 tbsp olive oil (divided)
- 1 3½-4-lb whole chicken
- 1½ oz pancetta, chopped into ¼-inch pieces

INSTRUCTIONS

1. Pat chicken dry with paper towels and season with salt inside and out.
2. Tie legs with kitchen twine. Let sit for 1 hr to allow salt to penetrate.
3. Place a rack in upper-third of the oven and set a 12" cast-iron skillet on a rack. Preheat oven to 425°.
4. In the meantime, toss onions, pancetta, squash and 2 tbsp oil in a bowl to coat; season with salt and pepper.
5. Pat dry chicken with paper towels and lightly coat with half of the remaining oil.
6. Drizzle remaining oil into hot skillet.
7. Carefully place chicken in the center of the skillet and arrange squash mixture around.
8. Roast until vegetables are golden brown and tender.
9. Let chicken rest in the skillet until slightly warm.
10. Transfer chicken into cutting board and carve.
11. Serve with vegetables.

Cornbread and Beef Skillet Pie

Prep time: 5 minutes
Cook time: 25 minutes
Total Time: 30 minutes
Serves: 4

INGREDIENTS

- 1 pound Lean Ground Beef
- 1 can corn kernels
- 1 package cornbread mix
- 2 oz. pepper jack cheese
- 1 can Ranchero Beans

INSTRUCTIONS

1. Heat oven to 400°.
2. In your oven-safe cast iron, cook the lean ground beef over medium-high heat, break it up using spoon until browned.
3. Add corn and beans then stir and cook.
4. Meanwhile, prepare the cornbread and follow package directions.
5. Spread the batter over the beef, leaving a ½ " border all the way around.
6. Sprinkle with cheese.
7. Bake for 20 minutes until golden brown.
8. Let cool.
9. Serve and enjoy!

Skillet Hash Browns

Prep time: 10 minutes
Cook time: 35 minutes
Total Time: 45 minutes
Serves: 6

INGREDIENTS
- 8 tbsp vegetable oil
- 5 russet potatoes (peeled, coarsely shredded)
- 1 ½ tsp kosher salt
- Coarse sea salt
- ¼ tsp pepper
- 2 bunches scallions, whites and greens are separated (sliced thinly)

INSTRUCTIONS

1. First, rinse the potatoes, drain and transfer to a bowl.
2. Add pepper and salt; toss to coat.
3. Heat the 6 tbsp of oil in a cast-iron skillet over medium-high heat.
4. Add half of the potatoes and press gently in an even layer.
5. Sprinkle with scallion whites and top with the remaining potatoes, then press again gently.
6. Cook for 10-15 mins. until golden brown.
7. Slide the hash browns onto a plate.
8. Place the cast-iron skillet upside down over the hash browns and then flip to invert; and browned side up.
9. Drizzle the remaining 2 tbsp of oil around the skillet.
10. Cook hash browns for another 10-15 minutes until the bottom is golden brown.
11. Slide onto a plate then season with sea salt.
12. Serve with scallion greens on top and then cut into wedges.

Frittata with Chorizo and Chard

Prep time: 2 minutes
Cook time: 15 minutes
Total Time: 17 minutes
Serves: 4

INGREDIENTS

- 1 tbsp olive oil
- 8 large eggs
- ¼ small onion (cut into halves)
- 1½ oz Manchego cheese (grated)
- 1 tbsp chopped fresh flat-leaf parsley
- 1 tbsp chopped chives
- salt and pepper
- 4 oz dried chorizo, thinly sliced
- 6 fingerling potatoes (thinly sliced)
- 1 bunch small chard, leaves coarsely chopped (ribs and stems removed)

INSTRUCTIONS

1. First, heat broiler.
2. In a large bowl, whisk eggs first, then cheese and herbs; season with salt and pepper.
3. Then cook chorizo in a 10" broiler proof cast-iron skillet over a medium heat. Stir often until browned and crisp. Transfer to the plate.
4. On the same cast-iron skillet, heat oil; put onion, season with salt. Cook and stir occasionally until it begins to soften.
5. Add potatoes and cook, tossing often until softened.
6. Add chard and cook. Stir often until chard is wilted. Season to taste with salt and pepper.
7. Mix in chorizo and pour in egg mixture. Tilt skillet to evenly distribute.
8. Cook for 2 minutes then transfer to oven and broil until egg is cooked and starting to brown for about 5 minutes.
9. Run a heatproof spatula around the edges of the frittata to loosen then slide onto the plate
10. Serve in wedges.

Pan-Roasted Chicken Thighs

Prep time: 5 minutes
Cook time: 32 minutes
Total Time: 37 minutes
Serves: 5

INGREDIENTS

- 6 chicken thighs
- 1 tbsp vegetable oil
- Kosher salt
- freshly ground pepper

INSTRUCTIONS

1. Preheat oven to 475 degrees.
2. Season the chicken to taste with salt and pepper.
3. Heat oil in your 12" cast-iron skillet over high heat.
4. Nestle chicken in cast-iron skillet, with the skin side down and then cook for 2 minutes.
5. Reduce the heat to medium-high. Continue to cook, still skin side down, rearranging the chicken thighs occasionally and tilting pan to distribute the heat until the fat renders and the skin turns to golden brown.
6. Transfer the skillet to oven and cook for 13 minutes more.
7. Flip the chicken. Continue to cook until skin becomes crisps and the meat is cooked through.
8. Transfer onto a plate. Let rest before serving.

Pan-Seared Sausage with Lady Apples and Watercress

Prep time: 5 minutes
Cook time: 30 minutes
Total Time: 35 minutes
Serves: 4

INGREDIENTS
- Kosher salt
- 1 tbsp olive oil
- freshly ground black pepper
- ¼ c dry white wine
- 1 lb lady apples (halved through stem ends)
- 1½ lb sweet Italian sausages
- 2 tbsp white wine vinegar
- 1 bunch watercress (trimmed)

INSTRUCTIONS

1. Heat oil in a cast-iron skillet over medium-high heat.
2. Put apples and then cook, turn occasionally until golden brown.
3. Prick sausages with a fork, add to skillet and then cook. Turn the sausages occasionally until browned.
4. Add vinegar and wine to skillet. Bring to boil.
5. Reduce the heat and then simmer until thickens.
6. Add watercress and toss to coat. Season to taste with salt and pepper.
7. Ready for serving

Apple Dutch Baby

Prep time: 5 minutes
Cook time: 29 minutes
Total Time: 34 minutes
Serves: 4

INGREDIENTS
apple cider syrup

- 4 c apple cider
- ½ tsp ground cinnamon
- 1 tsp vanilla extract
- 2 tbsp unsalted butter
- 1 tbsp light brown sugar

dutch baby

- 3 large eggs
- ¾ c whole milk
- ¾ c all-purpose flour
- ¼ tsp kosher salt
- 1 tsp vanilla extract
- 1 tsp ground cinnamon (divided)
- 1 tbsp light brown sugar
- 4 tbsp unsalted butter (divided)
- 1 large Lady apple (peeled, sliced ¼" thick)

INSTRUCTIONS

Apple cider syrup
1. In a large saucepan, bring butter, cinnamon, brown sugar, cider and vanilla to a boil over a medium-high heat.
2. Reduce heat and boil gently for 30-45 minutes. Stirring occasionally until thick and syrupy.

Dutch baby
1. Preheat oven to 425 degrees.
2. In a medium bowl, mix milk, vanilla, salt, flour eggs and 1 tsp cinnamon until smooth. Set aside.
3. Melt 2 tbsp butter in a 10" cast-iron skillet over medium heat.
4. Put apple and sprinkle brown sugar and remaining ½ tsp cinnamon.
5. Cook, tossing occasionally until apple is coated and softened. Transfer to a plate.
6. Wipeout cast-iron skillet and heat in oven until very hot.
7. Add remaining 2 tbsp butter, tilting to coat bottom and sides.
8. Add apple to the center of skillet; pour batter over.
9. Bake until pancake is already puffed and golden brown around edges and center is set but still custardy.
10. Serve drizzled with apple cider syrup.

Butternut Squash Shakshuka

Prep time: 4 minutes
Cook time: 38 minutes
Total Time: 42 minutes
Serves: 5

INGREDIENTS

- Kosher salt
- 1 28-oz can whole plum tomatoes with juices
- 3 tbsp olive oil
- 2 garlic cloves (finely chopped)
- 1 medium onion (finely chopped)
- ½ medium butternut squash (peeled, seeded, and cut into ½" pcs)
- freshly ground pepper
- 2 tsp ancho chile powder
- 2 tbsp sambal oelek
- 4 large eggs
- Cilantro leaves with tender stems (for serving)

INSTRUCTIONS

1. Preheat oven to 375 degrees.
2. Crush tomatoes with clean hands or potato masher in a bowl, then set aside.
3. Heat oil in a heat-proof skillet over medium.
4. Cook onion, squash, and garlic. Stir occasionally until tender.
5. Season to taste with salt and pepper, stir in chili powder and cook until fragrant.
6. Increase heat to medium-high, add sambal oelek and the reserved tomatoes, and then season to taste with salt and pepper.
7. Continue to cook. Stir until thickened.
8. Remove from heat.
9. Using the back of the spoon, make 4 depressions into the tomato mixture and then crack an egg into each.
10. Transfer to oven and bake shakshuka for about 12 minutes until yolks are slightly wobbling and egg whites are set when the pan is shaken.
11. Top shakshuka with cilantro and serve.

Skillet Roast Chicken with Parsnips, Scallions and Fennel

Prep time: 5 minutes
Cook time: 50 minutes
Total Time: 55 minutes
Serves: 6

INGREDIENTS

- Kosher salt
- freshly ground black pepper
- 3 tbsp olive oil (divided)
- 1 bunch scallions
- 1 3½-4-lb. chicken
- 1 fennel bulb (sliced lengthwise ½" thick)
- 2 large parsnips (peeled and sliced ½" thick on the diagonal)
- 3 wide strips lemon zest
- Lemon wedges (for serving)

INSTRUCTIONS

1. Preheat oven 425 degrees.
2. Heat 1 tbsp oil in a large ovenproof cast-iron skillet over medium-high.
3. Season the chicken in and out to taste with salt and pepper. Cook with breast side down until golden brown.
4. Use tongs to rotate the chicken. Don't tear the skin then brown all sides. Transfer to a plate and reserve skillet.
5. Toss fennel, scallions, lemon zest and parsnips in the skillet with the remaining 2 tbsp oil. Season to taste with salt and pepper.
6. Carefully place chicken on top of vegetables, breast side up.
7. Roast for about 40 minutes.
8. Transfer chicken to a cutting board and let rest before carving.
9. Serve with pan juices and spoon over lemon wedges.

Skillet Cornbread with Chives

Prep time: 2 minutes
Cook time: 30 minutes
Total Time:32 minutes
Serves: 8

INGREDIENTS

- 1 large egg
- 2 c coarse-grind cornmeal
- 1½ c buttermilk
- ½ c (1 stick) unsalted butter
- 1 tsp kosher salt
- ½ tsp baking powder
- ½ tsp baking soda
- 2 tbsp sugar (optional)
- 1 tbsp lard or vegetable oil
- 2 tbsp chives (finely chopped)
- Flaky sea salt (for serving)

INSTRUCTIONS

1. Carefully place a rack in the middle of the oven and set the cast-iron skillet on the rack. Preheat to 450°.
2. In the meantime, put sugar, cornmeal, baking powder, Kosher salt and baking soda in a large bowl.
3. In another bowl, combine egg and buttermilk. Add to dry ingredients and mix to incorporate.
4. Remove skillet from oven. Add lard and tilt pan to coat.
5. Scrape batter into skillet.
6. Bake cornbread for about 15-20 minutes until top is golden brown and center is firm.
7. Let cool before serving.
8. Spread butter over cornbread, top with chives and sprinkle with sea salt.

Rosemary Skillet Pork Chops with Quick Braised Cabbage

Prep time: 3 minutes
Cook time: 25 minutes
Total Time: 28 minutes
Serves: 4

INGREDIENTS

- 2 tsp sugar
- 3 tbsp olive oil
- 4 tbsp balsamic vinegar
- Kosher salt and pepper
- 4 small bone-in pork chops
- 8 small Garlic cloves
- 1 red onion
- 4 sprig fresh rosemary
- 1 small head red cabbage

INSTRUCTIONS

1. Heat oven to 425 degrees.
2. Heat 2 tbsp oil in a skillet over medium-high heat.
3. Season the pork chops with ½ tsp each of salt and pepper.
4. Cook on one side until golden brown.
5. Turn the chops and scatter garlic and rosemary around the chops. Cook for another 2 minutes.
6. Transfer your skillet to the oven and roast for 6 to 8 minutes until the chops are just cooked through.
7. Let the chops rest before serving.
8. In the meantime, heat remaining oil in a second skillet over medium heat.
9. Put the onion and ½ tsp each of salt and pepper. Cook for 5 minutes, covered, stirring occasionally.
10. Add the sugar, cabbage, 2 tbsp vinegar and 3 tbsp water and simmer, covered, until liquid has nearly evaporated and the cabbage is tender; add the remaining vinegar.
11. Serve with the garlic, pork chops, and rosemary.

One-Skillet Steak and Spring Veg with Spicy Mustard

Prep time: 3 minutes
Cook time: 25 minutes
Total Time: 28 minutes
Serves: 5

INGREDIENTS

- Kosher salt
- freshly ground pepper
- 1 lb boneless strip steak (patted dry)
- 5 garlic cloves (1 grated, 4 thinly sliced)
- 1 tbsp sherry vinegar
- 1 tsp honey
- 1-2 pinches cayenne pepper
- ⅓ c Dijon mustard
- ⅓ c plus 3 tbsp olive oil
- 1 bunch scallions (sliced, divided)
- 1 10-oz bag frozen peas
- 1 bunch asparagus (cut into 1" pieces)

INSTRUCTIONS

1. First, season steak all over with salt and pepper.
2. Put 1 grated garlic clove, 1 tsp honey, ⅓ c mustard, a couple pinches of cayenne, 1 tbsp vinegar, ⅓ c oil, and 1 tablespoon water in a bowl to combine.
3. Season to taste the spicy mustard with salt and pepper.
4. Heat a dry medium cast-iron skillet over medium-high.
5. Next, rub steak all over with 1 tablespoon oil and cook; turn every 2 minutes, until medium-rare about 10 minutes.
6. Carefully transfer steak to a plate and let sit.
7. Drain oil from skillet, leaving crispy bits behind.
8. Heat remaining 2 tbsp oil in the same skillet over low.
9. Add the 4 sliced garlic cloves and all 2 tbsp scallions and cook. Stir often until translucent and softened.
10. Add peas and water then cook. Stirring to break up slightly, until the peas are tender.
11. Add asparagus; season to taste with salt and pepper.
12. Cook and then stir often until asparagus is just tender.
13. Remove from heat.
14. Slice steak and shingle over the vegetables in skillet.
15. Drizzle some mustard sauce over steak and then top with reserved scallions.
16. Serve with the remaining mustard sauce alongside.

Classic Skillet Cornbread

Prep time: 4 minutes
Cook time: 30 minutes
Total Time: 34 minutes
Serves: 5

INGREDIENTS

- 1 large egg
- 2½ c coarse-grind cornmeal
- 1¼ tsp baking soda
- 1¼ tsp kosher salt
- 1⅔ c buttermilk
- 2 tbsp lard or unsalted butter
- hot honey butter (for serving)

INSTRUCTIONS

1. Preheat oven to 375°.
2. Set a dry cast-iron skillet over a low heat while you make the batter.
3. Put a baking soda, cornmeal, and salt in a bowl. Make a hole in the middle and add buttermilk and egg.
4. Beat vigorously starting in the middle to incorporate egg until the dry ingredients are well incorporated and the batter is already smooth.
5. Increase heat to medium-high and add lard or unsalted butter to skillet and then swirl to coat the bottom and sides.
6. Whisk batter again to incorporate then pour into cast-iron skillet and then smooth top.
7. Bake cornbread in an oven for 25-30 minutes until edges are golden brown, cracked in places, the top is golden and firm to touch.
8. Let cool in pan before cutting into wedges.
9. Serve with honey butter.

Cast-Iron Roast Chicken with Fennel and Carrots

Prep time: 10 minutes
Cook time: 100 minutes
Total Time: 110 minutes
Serves: 4

INGREDIENTS

- 1 3½ lb whole patted dry chicken
- 3 tbsp olive oil (divided)
- salt and pepper
- 2 fennel bulbs (cut into 6 wedges)
- 1 lb small carrots (peeled, cut into 4" long pieces diagonal)

INSTRUCTIONS

1. Season chicken with salt generously inside and out.
2. Tie legs together with kitchen twine.Let sit for 1 hour and let the salt penetrate.
3. Place a rack in the upper third of oven and set a 12 inches cast-iron skillet on rack.
4. Preheat oven to 425 degrees.
5. In the meantime, put carrots, fennel and 2 tbsp of oil in a large bowl to coat; season with pepper and salt.
6. Pat dry chicken with paper towels and coat with half of remaining oil.
7. Drizzle remaining oil into hot skillet. Place chicken in the center and arrange vegetables around after.
8. Roast for 50-60 minutes until fennel and the carrots are golden browned in spots and tender.
9. Insert the instant-read thermometer into the thickest part of breasts registers 155 degrees.
10. Let chicken rest in skillet for 20-40 minutes before transferring to a cutting board and then carve.
11. Serve with vegetables.

Pastrami and Potato Hash with Fried Eggs

Prep time: 3 minutes
Cook time: 46 minutes
Total Time: 49 minutes
Serves: 5

INGREDIENTS

- salt and pepper
- 4 large eggs
- 4 tbsp unsalted butter
- 4 tbsp olive oil (divided)
- 1½lb Yukon Gold potatoes (peeled, cut into 1" pcs)
- ½ lb winter squash (peeled, cut into 1" pcs)
- 2 leeks, white and pale-green parts only (chopped)
- 1 garlic clove (chopped)
- 1 lb pastrami
- ¼ c sliced chives

INSTRUCTIONS

1. First heat butter and 2 tbsp oil in a cast-iron skillet over medium-high heat.
2. Add potatoes and winter squash, season with salt and pepper; cook and stir occasionally until vegetables becomes tender.
3. Add garlic and leeks to hash and season with salt and pepper.
4. Lightly smash vegetables with the back of spatula or spoon.
5. Add pastrami and cook. Stir often until meat is warmed through and flavors have melded
6. Heat remaining oil in a cast-iron skillet over medium-high heat.
7. Crack eggs into skillet one at a time, and season with salt and pepper.
8. Cook until whites are set but yolks are still runny.
9. Divide hash among shallow bowls and top with an egg. Scatter chives over top.

Chocolate Dutch Baby

Prep time: 3 minutes
Cook time: 18 minutes
Total Time: 21 minutes
Serves: 2

INGREDIENTS

- 3 large eggs
- ⅓ c all-purpose flour
- ½ c whole milk
- ¼ c sugar
- ¼ c heavy cream
- 1 tbsp unsalted butter
- 3 tablespoon unsweetened cocoa powder
- ¾ tsp kosher salt (plus more)
- 1 oz bittersweet or milk chocolate
- Coffee ice cream (to serve)

INSTRUCTIONS

1. Arrange a rack in the center of oven, place a dry skillet on rack; preheat to 425 degrees.
2. Mix 3 eggs, ⅓ c flour, ¼ c sugar, 3 tbsp cocoa powder, and ¾ teaspoon salt in a bowl until smooth.
3. Beating constantly, slowly stream ½ c milk into egg mixture.
4. Cover and let the batter rest for about 15 minutes.
5. In the meantime, chop 1-ounce chocolate and transfer to a saucepan.
6. Add ¼ c cream and then cook over low heat, whisking occasionally, until chocolate is melted and the mixture is completely smooth. Season with a bit of salt and keep warm over low heat.
7. Remove skillet from oven and add a 1 tablespoon butter; tilt skillet to melt, make sure to coat the entire bottom and sides.
8. Give the batter a quick whisk to reincorporate, and then pour into the skillet.
9. Carefully transfer to oven.
10. Cook until pancake is puffed.
11. Remove the skillet from oven and let rest about 2 minutes.
12. Meanwhile, get ice cream out of the freezer.
13. Top with coffee ice cream and drizzle with your chocolate sauce.
14. Best serve if warm.

Skillet Shrimp, Sausage, and Rice

Prep time: 5 minutes
Cook time: 21 minutes
Total Time: 26 minutes
Serves: 4

INGREDIENTS

- 2 tsp Creole seasoning
- 2 tbsp olive oil
- 12 oz peeled and deveined shrimp
- 6 oz fully cooked andouille sausage
- 12 oz plum tomatoes
- 1 medium onion
- 1 red pepper
- 2 clove garlic
- 1 cup long-grain white rice
- 1/2 cup dry white wine
- 1 3/4 cup low-sodium chicken broth
- 1/2 cup fresh flat-leaf parsley

INSTRUCTIONS

1. Heat oil in a large skillet over medium-high heat.
2. Add the sausage and cook until browned. Transfer to a plate.
3. Reduce heat to medium, add onion and cook, covered, stirring occasionally, for 4 minutes.
4. Add the pepper and garlic and cook, occasionally stir, until the vegetables are just tender.
5. Stir in the rice, then the wine and seasoning and bring to a simmer.
6. Add the broth and boil.
7. Reduce heat and simmer, covered, for 12 minutes.
8. Fold the sausage into the rice mixture, nestle the shrimp in the partially cooked rice and cook, covered, until the shrimp are opaque throughout and the rice is tender, 4 to 5 minutes more.
9. Fold in the tomatoes and sprinkle with the parsley before serving.

One-Skillet Hot Sausage and Cabbage Stir-Fry with Chives

Prep time: 3 minutes
Cook time: 18 minutes
Total Time: 21 minutes
Serves: 4

INGREDIENTS

- 1 of 1" piece ginger (peeled, chopped)
- 4 garlic cloves (chopped)
- 1 lb hot Italian sausage (casings removed)
- 1 tsp toasted sesame oil
- 2 tsp sesame seeds
- 2 tbsp seasoned rice vinegar
- 2 tbsp soy sauce
- 2 tbsp vegetable oil (or more)
- 6 oz shiitake mushrooms (thinly sliced)
- 6 c Napa cabbage (very thinly sliced, divided)
- ⅓ c thinly sliced chives
- 8 large flour tortillas (warmed)
- Sriracha and Hoisin sauce (for serving)

INSTRUCTIONS

1. Work ginger and garlic into a sausage in a medium bowl; use a wooden spoon.
2. Heat 2 tablespoon vegetable oil in a large cast-iron skillet over medium-high and cook sausage mixture, until browned, crisp. break up with spoon and cooked through.
3. Transfer the mixture to a bowl.
4. Increase heat to high and cook mushrooms, then toss occasionally until turns brown and the juices are released.
5. Add half of the cabbage and cook. Toss often until wilted and tender.
6. Drizzle in soy sauce and vinegar and cook. Toss until liquid is reduced.
7. Remove skillet from heat and mix sausage, chives and remaining cabbage into a stir-fry.
8. Sprinkle with sesame seeds and drizzle with sesame oil.
9. Serve with tortillas, Sriracha, and hoisin sauce and individual wraps.

Olive Oil-Basted Fried Eggs

Prep time: 2 minutes
Cook time: 10 minutes
Total Time: 12 minutes
Serves: 2

INGREDIENTS

- 2 large eggs
- salt and pepper
- 3 tbsp olive oil

INSTRUCTIONS

1. Heat oil in a nonstick skillet over medium-high heat.
2. Add 1 egg at a time. Cook while shaking pan occasionally to avoid sticking together until the edges are golden brown.
3. Carefully tilt skillet and spoon oil that pools over the egg whites.
4. Transfer to a paper towel-lined plate to blot oil. Season to taste with salt and pepper.

Sambal Short Rib Stir-Fry

Prep time: 6 minutes
Cook time: 21 minutes
Total Time: 27 minutes
Serves: 5

INGREDIENTS

- 1 c basil leaves (torn)
- ¼ c sambal oelek
- 1 c low-sodium chicken broth
- 3 tbsp toasted sesame oil
- 1 tbsp mirin
- 1 lb boneless beef short ribs (sliced)
- salt and pepper
- 2 small onions (thinly sliced)
- 8 oz shiitake mushrooms (caps sliced, stems removed,)
- 1 bunch scallions (cut into 1" pcs)
- 1 2-inch piece ginger (peeled, chopped)
- 4 garlic cloves (grated)
- 6 medium radishes (trimmed, quartered)
- 6 oz snow peas
- Cooked short-grain rice (for serving)

INSTRUCTIONS

1. First, heat oil in a large cast-iron skillet over high heat.
2. Season beef with salt and pepper; cook, stirring occasionally until deeply browned.
3. It may seem wet at first but it will take on color and will look shiny.
4. Add onions and mushrooms; cook, tossing until they start to take on a little color and soften.
5. Add ginger, garlic, and scallions; cook, tossing constantly until slightly wilted.
6. Add sambal oelek and mirin; cook, tossing to coat.
7. put radishes, broth and snow peas and bring to boil.
8. Cook for 5 minutes until liquid is reduced by half. Meat and vegetables must be glossy and saucy.
9. Season to taste with salt and pepper.
10. Serve over rice and topped with basil.

Sweet Potato Kale Frittata

Prep time: 5 minutes
Cook time: 20 minutes
Total Time: 25 minutes
Serves: 5

INGREDIENTS

- 2 tbsp olive oil
- 6 large eggs
- 1 cup half-and-half
- 1 tsp salt
- ½ tsp pepper
- 2 c sweet potatoes
- 2 c firmly packed chopped kale
- ½ small red onion (chopped)
- 2 clove garlic (chopped)
- 3 oz. goat cheese

INSTRUCTIONS

1. Preheat oven to 350°.
2. Whisk together eggs, half-and-half, salt, and pepper in a bowl.
3. Sauté sweet potatoes in 1 tbsp hot oil in a 10" ovenproof nonstick skillet over medium heat until potatoes are golden and tender
4. Transfer to a plate and keep warm.
5. Sauté kale, red onion and garlic in remaining 1 tbsp oil until kale is tender and wilted; stir in potatoes.
6. Pour the egg mixture over vegetables, and cook for 3 minutes.
7. Sprinkle the egg mixture with goat cheese.
8. Bake at 350° for about 10-14 minutes or until set.
9. Cut into wedges and serve.

Herb-Garlic Crusted Flank Steak with Pan-Roasted Grapes

Prep time: 5 minutes
Cook time: 14 minutes
Total Time: 19 minutes
Serves: 4

INGREDIENTS

- 1 ½ tsp salt
- ¾ tsp pepper
- 2 tsp fresh thyme
- 2 tsp fresh rosemary
- 2 tbsp olive oil
- 2 tablespoon white balsamic vinegar
- 1 large garlic clove
- 1 flank steak
- 3 cup assorted whole grapes
- 2 shallots
- ½ cup freshly crumbled blue cheese

INSTRUCTIONS

1. Mix all amount of thyme, rosemary, garlic, salt and pepper in a bowl.
2. Rub the steak with herb mixture.
3. Heat 1 tablespoon oil in a large skillet over medium-high heat.
4. Cook steak until the desired degree of doneness.
5. Transfer and cover with foil loosely.
6. Reduce to medium heat.
7. Add remaining oil and sauté shallots and grapes until grapes just begin to soften.
8. Remove from heat and let sit for 1 minute.
9. Stir in vinegar and season to taste with salt and pepper.
10. Cut steak into thin slices.
11. Transfer to a serving platter, spooning cheese and grapes over meat.
12. If desired, sprinkle additional fresh herbs. Best served with mashed potatoes.

Seared Grouper with Corn, Zucchini, and Tomato Saute

Prep time: 3 minutes
Cook time: 10 minutes
Total Time: 13 minutes
Serves: 4

INGREDIENTS

- 1 tsp salt
- ½ tsp epper
- 2 tbsp olive oil
- 2 tbsp cold butter
- 4 grouper fillets or salmon (or other firm fish)
- 1 large shallot
- 2 medium zucchini
- 2 clove garlic (chopped)
- 1 ½ c cherry tomatoes
- 1/4 c torn basil leaves
- 1 1/2 c fresh yellow corn kernels

INSTRUCTIONS

1. Sprinkle fish with salt and pepper.
2. Heat oil in your nonstick cast-iron over medium-high heat.
3. Cook fish on each side until cooked through.
4. Transfer in a plate and keep it warm.
5. Sauté zucchini and shallot until crisp-tender.
6. Stir in corn and garlic, and sauté for 2 more minutes.
7. Reduce heat to low, and stir in butter, tomatoes, and basil; cook until butter is melted.
8. Season to taste with salt and pepper.
9. Spoon vegetables onto serving plate; top with fish.

VEGETABLE STIR FRY

Prep time: 10 minutes
Cook time: 30 minutes
Total Time: 40 minutes
Serves: 4

INGREDIENTS
Sauce:

- ¼ c orange marmalade
- ¼ c brown sugar
- 1 tbsp vegetable oil
- 2 tbsp soy sauce
- 1 tbsp sriracha
- 1 tbsp garlic (finely chopped)
- 2 tbsp ginger (finely chopped)
- 2 tbsp rice vinegar
- 2 tbsp cornstarch

For the stir fry:

- 1/4 c vegetable oil (divided)
- 2 c mushrooms (sliced into 1/4 inch pieces)
- 1 10 oz bag snow peas
- 1 yellow onion (sliced into 1/4 inch pieces)
- 4 large carrots (sliced into 1/4 inch pieces)
- 1/2 of a large Napa cabbage (shredded into 1/4 inch strips)
- 1 can water chestnuts (drained, patted dry)

INSTRUCTIONS

1. Combine all ingredients for sauce in a small bowl and stir.
2. While chopping vegetables preheat cast-iron mini wok over medium-high for 10 minutes.
3. When everything is ready, turn heat to high and add 1 tbsp oil to the wok.
4. Stir-fry onions and carrots until soft and are charred on the edges.
5. Transfer carrots and onions in a plate.
6. Add another tbsp of oil and put mushrooms with a pinch of salt; cook until reduced by half and golden brown. Transfer to another plate.
7. Add snow peas and cook until just charred and transfer to another plate.
8. Put the remaining oil, add whites of cabbage and cook for 3-4 minutes. Add greens and cook for 2 minutes more. Transfer to another plate.
9. Add sauce and stir continuously until reduced by half, then return all vegetables to the wok.
10. Toss to coat and add water chestnuts.
11. Serve immediately over rice.

GARLIC-TOPPED FLANK STEAK ROULADE

Prep time: 8 minutes
Cook time: 30 minutes
Total Time: 38 minutes
Serves: 4-6

INGREDIENTS
- Sea salt
- 2 plb grass-fed flank steak
- freshly ground black pepper
- 4 strips cooked pork bacon, chopped (but not crispy)
- 2 c loosely packed organic spinach leaves (chopped)
- 1/3 c organic sun-dried tomatoes (chopped)
- 1 c chopped organic button mushrooms
- 2 tbsp coconut oil
- 5 organic garlic cloves (minced)

INSTRUCTIONS

1. Preheat oven to 425°.
2. Pound the flank steak to an even ⅓ inch thickness with a meat mallet.
3. Season steak with salt and pepper on both sides to taste then lay it out flat in front of you.
4. Sprinkle chopped bacon over it in a single layer only. Then evenly layer on the spinach, tomatoes and mushrooms.
5. Roll the steak up lengthwise tightly into a log (roulade) and tie with a kitchen twine in 2 or 3 places to hold it together.
6. Heat the oil in a 12" cast-iron skillet over medium high heat.
7. Sear roulade until browned on all sides.
8. Remove pan from the heat and sprinkle garlic all over the roulade.
9. Place skillet in the oven until stuffing is hot but the meat is still pink in the center. A total of 10-15 minutes.
10. Remove from oven after and let rest for 10 minutes.
11. Remove twine and slice into pinwheels. Serve.

Skillet Shrimp Tacos

Prep time: 10 minutes
Cook time: 20 minutes
Total Time: 30 minutes
Serves: 4

INGREDIENTS

- 2 tsp grated lime zest
- 2 tbsp freshly squeezed lime juice
- 4 cup thinly sliced red cabbage
- 12 oz small shrimp
- 1/4 cup fresh cilantro
- 2 tbsp canola oil
- sour cream
- Hot pepper sauce
- Lime wedges

INSTRUCTIONS

1. Mix cabbage and lime juice in a large bowl.
2. In a separate bowl, combine shrimp with cilantro and lime zest.
3. Heat canola oil in 12" skillet over medium-high until very hot; add shrimp in single layer.
4. Cook until opaque throughout.
5. Transfer after cooking
6. Serve shrimp in flour tortillas with cabbage mixture, sour cream, hot pepper sauce, and lime wedges, if desired.

FESTIVE GOOD LUCK CORNBREAD SKILLET

Prep time: 10 minutes
Cook time: 55 minutes
Total Time: 65 minutes
Serves: 8

INGREDIENTS

Filling

- 1 lb smoked sausage (cut into 1/4 inch slices lengthwise)
- 1/2 tsp hot pepper sauce
- 1/2 c chopped onion
- 1 to 2 cloves garlic (finely minced)
- 2 (15 oz) cans drained black-eyed peas
- 1 14 1/2 oz can low-sodium chicken broth
- 1 10 oz package frozen collard greens (thawed, chopped)

Cornbread Topping

- 1 egg (beaten)
- 2 tsp sugar
- 1/4 c oil
- 2 c Martha White Self-Rising Cornmeal Mix
- 1 1/3 c buttermilk
- 1/4 c finely chopped fresh parsley or cilantro
- 1/2 c shredded cheddar cheese

INSTRUCTIONS

1. Preheat oven to 400°.
2. Cook sausage, onion and garlic in a 12" cast-iron skillet over medium-high heat until sausage is browned.
3. Add the remaining filling ingredients and stir, bring to boil, reduce the heat and simmer for about 10 minutes.
4. Combine all cornbread topping in a large bowl; stirring continuously until smooth.
5. Spoon the batter, spreading evenly over sausage mixture in the skillet.
6. Bake for 40 minutes or until the cornbread is browned.

Made in the USA
Monee, IL
07 July 2026

56546408R00059